New York, New York

by John Emmett Connors

On the cover: The Morningstar Diner
Opposite: Subway, Cooper Union Square

New York, New York
Copyright © 2009 by John Connors

All rights Reserved. No part of this book may be used or reproduced in any manner whatsoever without written permission from the author except in the case of brief quotation embodied in critical articles and reviews.

To order additional copies of this title, contact your favorite local bookstore or visit www.tbmbooks.com

Cover & Book design by Karen Schlesinger, Digital Artist's Space
Printed in the United States of America

The Troy Book Makers
www.thetroybookmakers.com

ISBN: 978-1-933994-9-70

For more information on the availability of original works and prints by John Connors please contact:

The Clement Frame Shop & Art Gallery
201 Broadway, Troy, NY 12180
1-888-876-9691
www.clementart.com

John Connors Website:
www.johnconnorspaintings.com

I came from Troy, NY to live in New York City in 1968, but due to the draft I did not stay long. After four years as a Navy hospital corpsman, I returned to the city and picked up where I left off. I studied at the Art Students League of New York with Robert Beverly Hale. At the same time I took lessons in sumi-e at the School of KoHo and did a brief stint at the Edo Cultural Center in Tokyo, Japan. I also spent one summer at Malden Bridge near Albany, NY, studying color with the portrait painter Betty Warren.

Some of the scenes in this book no longer exist, but many are more recent. Sometimes I paint recognizable landmarks, but more often I look to the lesser known places that are the heart, soul and guts of this city.

I hope you enjoy looking at these scenes as much as I have enjoyed painting them.

NEW YORK, NEW YORK

St. Paul the Apostle Church,
59th Street and 9th Avenue

Museum of Natural History

Chess Players, Central Park

Working on St. Paul's Church

Trump Tower and AT&T Buildings Under Construction

View of Empire State Building

The Music Box

St. Clements Church, W. 46th Street

Epstein's Paint Store, 9th Avenue

9th Avenue at 56th Street

9th Avenue at 57th Street

19th Street & 6th Avenue, Looking SW

NEW YORK, NEW YORK

W. 57th Street Pier

Penn Station

Broadway Looking Towards 72nd Street

Carnegie Hall

59th Street Bridge

Old Columbus Circle

All Night Store, 57th Street and 9th Avenue

Power Station, 10th Avenue

Highway Ramp, W. 56th Street

10th Avenue Car Wash

Manhattan Collision, Chelsea

W. 42nd Street Busses

God's Lighthouse, 8th Avenue, West Village

West Side Trucks

Taxi Graveyard, West Side

West Village Apartments

Keller's Bar, West Village

Ship near the end of Christopher Street

Boats near Christopher Street

Jane Street Hotel

Church and Pizza, Christopher Street

Prince Lumber

Manhattan Industrial Center

Old West Side Highway

Pier at Night

14th Street & 9th Avenue

St. Brigid's, across from Tompkin's Square Park, East Village

Little House in West Village

Nick's Barber Shop, West Village

The One Potato

Tompkins Square Market, East Village

New Jersey View I

New Jersey View II

Arthur's Tavern, West Village

West Street View of Old Post Office Building

Old Wooden House, E. 29th Street

East Village Cafe

Strand Bookstore

Psychic Reading, E. 25th Street

Williamsburg Bridge I

Williamsburg Bridge II

Under the Brooklyn Bridge I

NEW YORK, NEW YORK

Under the Brooklyn Bridge II

Katz's Deli

Silver Monuments, 125 Forsyth Street

Grand Street

Chinatown View

Under Bridge, Chinatown

Old Yankee Stadium

Gansvoort Garbage Towers

View From Brooklyn

*Thanks to everyone who has helped on this project:
Clement's Frame Shop & Art Gallery, Digital Artist's Space,
and my friends and family.*

For more information on the availability of original works and prints by John Connors please contact:

The Clement Frame Shop & Art Gallery
201 Broadway
Troy, NY 12180
Toll Free 1-888-Troy-NY-1
www.clementart.com

John Connors Website:
www.johnconnorspaintings.com